The Easter Angels

For Sam B.H.
For Matthew and Abbi T.J.

THE EASTER ANGELS

Bob Hartman
Illustrations by Tim Jonke

A LION BOOK

 The angel sat in the dark, and waited.

This was the most unusual assignment he had ever received. Up till now, his missions had always been straightforward—keeping children from falling into wells, helping lost travellers find their way. Typical guardian angel stuff.

But this job was different—a quick beam of light to mark the location, and a strange set of orders that simply said he should wait for his partner to arrive. Partner? He'd never had a partner before. So he couldn't help wondering what this was all about.

And then the angel saw something.

 T he sun reached one long finger over the horizon and, sure enough, there was someone coming towards him, wading through the darkness as if it were a thick, black sea. Could this be his partner? If so, it was the most unusual angel he had ever seen.

No song. No shimmer. No shine. There was hardly a hint of heaven about him. Instead, he was thin and tired—a small grey mouse of an angel.

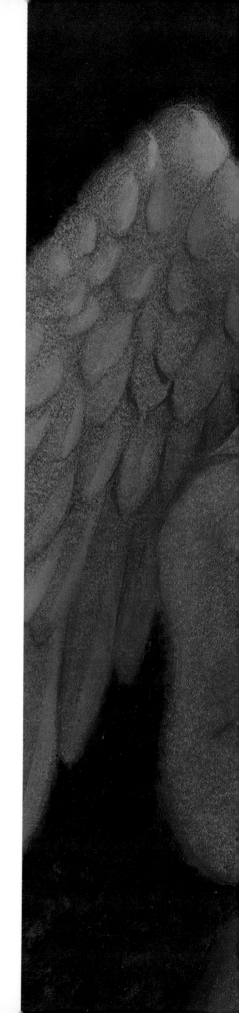

The first angel raised his hand, in a greeting. "Hello," he said. "My name is Candriel. Who are you?"

The second angel sat down beside his partner, but it was a minute or two before he spoke. And when he did, it was in a mouse's whisper that matched his looks.

"My name is Shakkath," he said solemnly. "I am the Angel of Death."

An early morning breeze blew past the angels, but it was not the breeze that made Candriel shiver. He'd heard of this angel. Everyone had. How he'd killed the Pharaoh's first-born son. How he'd slain, single-handed, an army of Assyrian soldiers in just one night. But to look at him, now, sitting there all small and grey and quiet, it hardly seemed possible.

Could this really be the Angel of Death? Candriel wondered. And what kind of mission was this going to be?

 "I suppose you have the orders?" said Candriel uncertainly.

Shakkath laid a bony hand on his pocket. "I do," he nodded. "But I was told not to open them until we saw women coming up the hill. It's got something to do with a secret—a surprise."

A partner. A signal. A surprise, thought Candriel. This job gets stranger and stranger. But all he dared say was, "What do you suppose the orders are?"

The Angel of Death shook his head. "Oh, that's not hard to guess. All you have to do is look around."

The sun's bright scalp edged over the horizon. And Candriel looked.

They were sitting in the middle of a graveyard!

"Death again," Shakkath sighed. "It seems as if death is always part of the job for me. So it makes sense that I should play some part in this one too—the saddest death of all."

Candriel looked again. The sun was a little higher, now, and he could see it all clearly. The garden graveyard. The sleeping soldiers. The city of Jerusalem in the distance.

"So you've guessed who's in the tomb we're sitting on?" asked Shakkath.

"Jesus," whispered Candriel. "It's Jesus, isn't it?"

A soldier grunted in his sleep. A bird whistled in the distance. And the Angel of Death just nodded.

"I saw it happen, you know," said Candriel, after a while. "Our whole battalion was ready to burst through the sky, uproot that cross, and save him. But they said the signal had to come from him. And the signal never came."

"I didn't watch," admitted Shakkath. "I couldn't. I'd seen too much death already. I'm sure he had a reason. He must have. But even that couldn't ease the terrible hurt."

"No," agreed Candriel. "He suffered a lot. They did some awful things to him."

"That's not what I mean," said Shakkath. "I mean the other kind of hurt that comes with death. Saying goodbye to your friends, to the ones you love. They say that even his mother was there."

Candriel looked puzzled.

"You're a guardian angel, aren't you?" asked Destroyer. "Big and strong—the rescuing type."

"Right," said Candriel. "And I'm good at what I do."

"I'm sure you are," said the Angel of Death. "And I'm also sure you feel a great deal of joy and gratitude from the people you save."

"Oh yes!" Candriel smiled.

"Well, it's different when you're the Angel of Death. Take the Assyrian army, for example. They had Jerusalem surrounded. They were going to kill the people inside. And it was my job to stop them."

"That must have been difficult," Candriel interrupted. "To kill so many of them. I mean, with you being so small."

Shakkath slowly shook his head. "No," he sighed. "Doing the job was the easy part. A quick breath in the face. That's all it took. Then their eyes glazed over and their hearts grew still.

"The hard part was the thoughts—those thousands and thousands of sad, goodbye thoughts:

My wife... I'll never see you again.
I'm sorry, Mother. I promised you I would come back.
Grow up well, my son…
I will miss you.

"Missing. Death is all about missing. That's what I remember most about that night. And that's what I think must have been so hard for Jesus and his friends."

Candriel looked at his partner. And what he saw was sadness. Sadness like some great thick shell that seemed to crush and shrink Shakkath.

"I just wish," Shakkath concluded, "I just wish that once I could have a mission where I remembered not sadness and loss, but the kind of joy and gratitude that you have felt so often."

Candriel didn't know what to say. But he was a guardian angel, after all. So at least he knew what to do. He opened up one glowing golden wing, wrapped it around the Angel of Death, and together they sat, in the sadness and the new day's light.

And that's when Candriel spotted the women.

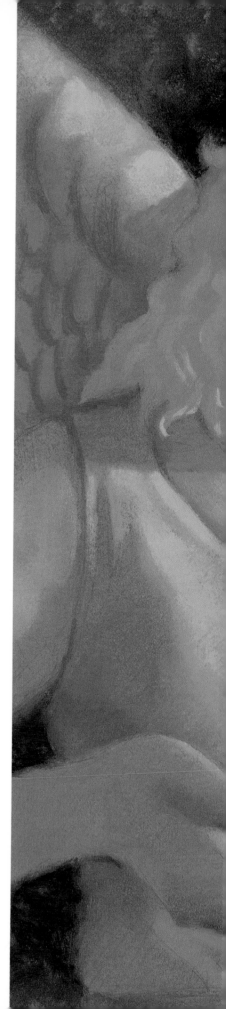

"That's the signal," he said. "It's time to read our orders." Shakkath reached into his pocket and handed the scroll to his partner. "You read it," he shuddered.

"There's nothing to worry about," Candriel said as he took the scroll. "We're probably supposed to protect these women from the soldiers. It's going to be all right. You'll see."

 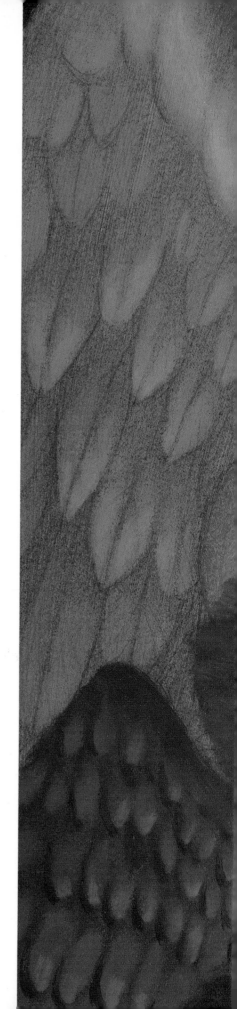

And, unrolling the scroll he read it out loud.

"Candriel," the orders said, "Guardian Angel, kind and strong. You wanted so badly to free my son from his cross. But that was not within your power. What is now within your power is to roll away the stone. Open his tomb and show the world that the one who died on the cross is now alive—free from death, for ever!

"As for you, Shakkath, faithful servant, Angel of Death, someone needs to tell these women that the one they miss is alive. Who better to share this joyful news than the one who best understands their sadness and loss?"

It took hardly a second. Candriel dropped the orders, leaped off the tomb, and rolled away the stone.

Shakkath was right behind, climbing down after him into the grave. It was empty.

It was empty!

And that's when Candriel saw his partner change.

The soldiers said it was an earthquake. They said they saw a flash of lightning.

But Candriel knew different.

The sound that cracked the morning stillness was a sad whisper exploding into a shout of joy. And the light that stunned the soldiers was a grim grey shadow bursting bright to white.

"He is not here!" Shakkath shouted to the women. "He is risen! He's alive!"

And the Angel of Death became, forevermore, the Angel of Life.

Text copyright © 1993 Bob Hartman
Illustrations copyright © 1999 Tim Jonke
This edition copyright © 1999 Lion Publishing

The moral rights of the author and illustrator
have been asserted

Published by
Lion Publishing plc
Sandy Lane West, Oxford, England
ISBN 0 7459 3877 9
www.lion-publishing.co.uk
Lion Publishing
4050 Lee Vance View, Colorado Springs, CO 80918, USA
ISBN 0 7459 3868 X

First edition 1999
10 9 8 7 6 5 4 3 2 1 0

This story has been adapted from "The Angel of Death
and Life", first published in *Angels, Angels All Around*
by Lion Publishing

A catalogue record for this book is available
from the British Library

Library of Congress CIP data applied for

Typeset in 14/21 Baskerville
Printed and bound in Singapore